THE FO

THE FOUNDATION STONE MEDITATION

RUDOLF STEINER

*Three translations and the original German,
with an introduction by Michael Wilson*

RUDOLF STEINER PRESS

Rudolf Steiner Press
Hillside House, The Square
Forest Row RH18 5ES

www.rudolfsteinerpress.com

Published by Rudolf Steiner Press 2005

The material in this book is extracted from *The Foundation Stone / The Life, Nature and Cultivation of Anthroposophy* (Rudolf Steiner Press 1996). The complete text of the Foundation Stone Meeting can be found in *The Christmas Conference for the Foundation of the General Anthroposophical Society 1923/1924* (Anthroposophic Press / Rudolf Steiner Press 1990). The original German texts can be found in *Die Weihnachtstagung zur Begründung der Allgemeinen Anthroposophischen Gesellschaft 1923/24* (volume 260 in the *Rudolf Steiner Gesamtausgabe* or Collected Works), Rudolf Steiner Verlag, Dornach. This authorized translation is published by permission of the Rudolf Steiner Nachlassverwaltung, Dornach

This translation © Rudolf Steiner Press 2005

All rights reserved. No part of this publication may be reproduced, stored in a retrieval system, or transmitted, in any form or by any means, electronic, mechanical, photocopying or otherwise, without the prior permission of the publishers

A catalogue record for this book is available from the British Library

ISBN 1 85584 173 8

Cover by Andrew Morgan
Typeset by DP Photosetting, Aylesbury, Bucks.
Printed and bound in the UK by 4edge Limited

Contents

Introduction by Michael Wilson *1*

Note by Rudolf Steiner *5*

THE FOUNDATION STONE MEDITATION

Translated by George Adams *9*

Alternative translation by Pauline Wehrle *17*

Alternative translation by Richard Seddon *25*

The Original German *33*

Further Reading *41*

Introduction

This 'Foundation Stone' of the Anthroposophical Society was formed at the Christmas Conference 1923 out of the tragedy a year earlier when the original Goetheanum building had gone up in flames during the last hour of 1922. The foundation stone of that building had been laid into the hill of Dornach during the stormy evening of 20 September 1913. It was a symbol of a deed which was to give visible and tangible form to the creative spirit of the world. The 'stone' consisted of a double pentagon-dodecahedron, made of copper. It was laid in an orientation with the larger of the two forms towards the east where the smaller dome of the building would later stand, and with the smaller form towards the larger dome of the building which would later house the auditorium. To this day it lies buried in its original concrete which now forms part of the foundations of the present building.

Reflection upon the geometrical attributes of the dodecahedron will show how the original foundation stone lives again in the Foundation Stone verses contained in this book. But the original building itself—half temple, half theatre—could not be repeated. World events made it impossible for it to arise again in any place other than the hearts of human beings. Only there can the human spirit now meet the spirit of the world, and the path along which this may happen is the path of anthroposophy.

It was early in 1913, when a first Anthroposophical Society emerged from the Theosophical Movement, that Rudolf Steiner described how the cosmic wisdom, the heavenly Sophia, had united herself with the evolution of human consciousness—'Philo-Sophia'—and now appeared once more, this time on earth in an objective form: 'Anthropos-Sophia'. This is not a wisdom that can be possessed; but the higher being which slumbers in every one of us can awaken and unite with the Being of Anthroposophia. The verses of this Foundation Stone are a call to us to bring about this awakening, a deed that can take place only within the free human individuality. This new individuality must turn its powers of recognition towards all that the gods have created for it and which makes its life possible, and it must direct its creative will towards the exploration of what awaits it in the spirit. In the balance of the two the individual will find its true humanity.

In working with this meditation we should not forget that when it was originally heard, on Christmas morning 1923, it was the first half of each of the three verses that constituted 'our Foundation Stone', whereas the second halves, which are the Cosmic Reply, came a little later. In this sense the dialogue between the human spirit and the spirit of the world reveals a dramatic depth of meaning.

*

Since it is seldom possible to convey the original mantric quality in a single translation, we have included more than one here, in the hope that serious students will work with the one which they find most helpful in leading them towards the original mantric content.

When this content is fully understood it will be seen to be a milestone in human evolution on earth.

Michael Wilson
1979*

---

* The complete text of this introduction can be found in *The Foundation Stone* (Rudolf Steiner Press 1996).

Note by Rudolf Steiner

Explanatory words relating to the text of the Foundation Stone Verses printed for members in the Nachrichtenblatt *(Members' News-sheet) of 13 January 1924.*

In close connection with the opening meeting was the ceremony on the morning of 25 December, which we entitled 'Laying of the Foundation Stone of the Anthroposophical Society'.

It could only be a question of laying a Foundation Stone in an ideal and spiritual sense. The ground in which the Stone was laid was none other than the hearts and souls of those united in the Society, and the Foundation Stone itself must be the mood and spirit springing of its own accord from the anthroposophical way of life.

This mood and spirit, so evidently called for by all the signs of the present time, lives in the will to find—by deepening the human soul—the path to an awakened vision of the spirit and to a life proceeding from the spirit. I will now put down the verses in which I tried to give shape to this 'Foundation Stone'.

THE FOUNDATION STONE MEDITATION

Translated by George Adams (1927)

Soul of Man!
Thou livest in the limbs
Which bear thee through the world of Space
Into the ocean-being of the Spirit.
Practise *Spirit-recollection*
In depths of soul,
Where in the strength sublime
Of world-creative life
Thine own I grows to full being
In the I of God.
Then in the being of the World of Man
Thy *Life* will be true.

For the Father-Spirit of the Heights
Reigns in the depths of the World, begetting life.
Spirits of Strength!
May there ring forth from the Heights
The call that is re-echoed in the Depths,
Saying:
From the Divine springeth Mankind.
Spirit-beings hear it in East and West and North and South:
May human beings hear it!

Soul of Man!
Thou livest in the beat of heart and lung
Which guides thee through the rhythm of the
   Ages
Into the feeling of thine own Soul-being.
Practise *Spirit-meditation*
In the balance of the soul,
Where the surging deeds
Of cosmic evolution
Unite thine own I
With the I of the World.
Then in the working of the Soul of Man
Thy *Feeling* will be true.

For the Christ-Will in this horizon's Round
Reigns in the rhythms of the World, blessing the soul.
Spirits of Light!
May there be kindled from the East
The flame that is moulded by the West,
Saying:
In Christ Death becomes Life.
Spirit-beings hear it in East and West and North and South:
May human beings hear it!

Soul of Man!
Thou livest in the resting head
Which from the wellsprings of Eternity
Unlocks for thee the Thoughts of the World.
Practise *Spirit-penetration*
In restfulness of thought,
Where the eternal aims of God
Grant light of cosmic being
To thine own I
For free and active Will.
Then in the spiritual founts of Man
Thy *Thought* will be true.

For the Cosmic Thoughts of the Spirit
Reign in the being of the World, praying for
 light.
Spirits of Soul!
May there ascend from the Depths
The prayer that is heard in the Heights,
Saying:
In the cosmic Spirit-Thoughts the Soul awakes.
Spirit-beings hear it in East and West and North
 and South:
May human beings hear it!

At the turning-point of time,
The Spirit-Light of the World
Entered the stream of Earthly Evolution.
Darkness of Night
Had held its sway;
Day-radiant Light
Poured into the souls of men:
Light that gave warmth
To simple shepherds' hearts,
Light that enlightened
The wise heads of kings.

O Light Divine!
O Sun of Christ!
Warm Thou our hearts,
Enlighten Thou our heads,
That good may become
What from our hearts we would found
And from our heads direct
With single purpose.

Alternative translation by Pauline Wehrle

Human Soul!
You live in the limbs
Which bear you through the world of space
Within the flowing ocean of the spirit:
Practise *spirit re-cognition*
In depths of soul,
Where in the wielding will
Of world creating
The individual I
Comes to being
In the I of God;
And you will truly *live*
In your body's cosmic being.

For the Father Spirit of the heights is present
In world depths begetting existence:
Spirits of Strength!
May there ring forth from the heights
The call re-echoed in the depths;
Proclaiming:
Humankind is born of God.
The elemental spirits hear it
In east, west, north, south:
*May hu*man beings *hear it!*

Human Soul!
You live in the beat of heart and lung
Which leads you through the rhythm of time
Into the realm of your own soul's feeling.
Practise *spirit presence*
In soul composure,
Where the weaving deeds
Of universal becoming
Unite
The individual I
With the I of the World;
And you will truly *feel*
In the active life of your soul.

For the Christ Will is present all around
In world rhythms shedding grace on our souls;
Spirits of Light!
May what is formed by the west
Have been quickened in the light of the east;
Proclaiming:
In Christ death becomes life.
The elemental spirits hear it
In east, west, north, south:
*May hu*man beings *hear it!*

Human Soul!
You live in the stillness of the head
Which from the founts of eternity
Discloses for you cosmic thoughts:
Practise *spirit beholding*
In thought calm,
Where the eternal aims of Gods
Give the light of spirit worlds
To the individual I
For will in freedom.
And you will truly *think*
In the founts of your human spirit.

For the Spirit's cosmic thoughts are present
In world existence begging for light;
Spirits of Soul!
May there ascend from the depths
The plea heard in the heights;
Proclaiming:
In the Spirit's cosmic thoughts the soul will
    awaken.
The elemental spirits hear it
In east, west, north, south:
*May hu*man beings *hear it!*

At the turning of time
Cosmic Spirit Light descended
Into the earthly stream of being;
Darkness of night
Had run its course;
The light of day
Shone forth in human souls:
Light
That gives warmth
To poor shepherds' hearts,
Light
That enlightens
The wise heads of kings.

God-given light,
Christ Sun
Give warmth
To our hearts;
Give light
To our heads;
That what we found
From our hearts
What we guide
From our heads
Will be good.

Alternative translation by Richard Seddon

Soul of Man!
You live within the limbs
Which bear you through the world of Space
Into the ocean-being of the spirit:
Practise *spirit-remembering*
In depths of soul,
Where in the sovereign
World-Creator presence
One's own I
Within God's I
Gains Being;
And you shall truly *live*
In cosmic Being of Man.

For the Father Spirit of the heights holds sway
In the depths of worlds begetting existence:
Spirits of Power
Let from the heights ring out
What in the depths is echoed;
This resounds:
From the Divine mankind has Being.
> This the spirits hear in East, West, North, South;
> May men hear it.

Soul of Man!
You live within the beat of heart and lung
Which leads you through the rhythms of Time
Into your own soul-nature's weaving feelings:
Practise *spirit-awareness*
In balance of the soul,
Where the on-surging
Deeds of world-becoming
One's own I
And I of world
Unite;
And you shall truly *feel*
In the soul-working of Man.

For the Will of Christ all around holds sway
In the world rhythms bestowing grace on souls:
Spirits of Light!
Let from the East flame up
What through the West takes form;
This resounds:
In Christ death becomes life.*
> This the spirits hear in East, West, North, South;
> May men hear it.

---

* May also be read: In Christ life becomes death. (In Christo morimur—In Christ we die.)

Soul of Man!
You live within the resting head
Which from the grounds of eternity
Reveals the universal thoughts:
Practise *spirit-beholding*
In the calm of thought,
Where the eternal aims of Gods
World-Being's light
On one's own I
Bestow
For will in freedom;
And you shall truly *think*
In spirit foundations of Man.

For the spirit's cosmic thoughts hold sway
In world Being beseeching light:
Spirits of Soul!
Let from the depths be entreated
What in the heights finds hearing;
This resounds:
In the Spirits cosmic thoughts the soul awakes.
> This the spirits hear in East, West, North, South;
> May men hear it.

At the turning of the times
Cosmic Spirit Light descended
Into the earthly stream of Being:
Darkness of night
Had run its course;
Day-bright light
Shone forth in human souls;
Light
That brings warmth
To simple shepherds' hearts;
Light
That illumines
The wise heads of kings.

Godly Light,
Christ Sun,
Set aglow
Our hearts,
Illuminate
Our heads,
That good may be
What we
From hearts would found,
What we
From heads would guide,
In steadfast will.

The Original German

Menschenseele!
Du lebest in den Gliedern,
Die dich durch die Raumeswelt
In das Geistesmeereswesen tragen:
Übe Geist-Erinnern
In Seelentiefen,
Wo in waltendem
Weltenschöpfer-Sein
Das eigne Ich
Im Gottes-Ich
Erweset;
Und du wirst wahrhaft *leben*
Im Menschen-Welten-Wesen.

Denn es waltet der Vater-Geist der Höhen
In den Weltentiefen Sein-erzeugend.
Ihr Kräfte-Geister
Lasset aus den Höhen erklingen,
Was in den Tiefen das Echo findet;
Dieses spricht:
Aus dem Göttlichen weset die Menschheit.
Das hören die Geister in Ost, West, Nord, Süd:
Menschen mögen es hören.

Menschenseele!
Du lebest in dem Herzens-Lungen-Schlage,
Der dich durch den Zeitenrhythmus
Ins eigne Seelenwesensfühlen leitet:
Übe *Geist-Besinnen*
Im Seelengleichgewichte,
Wo die wogenden
Welten-Werde-Taten
Das eigne Ich
Dem Welten-Ich
Vereinen;
Und du wirst wahrhaft *fühlen*
Im Menschen-Seelen-Wirken.

Denn es waltet der Christus-Wille im Umkreis
In den Weltenrhythmen Seelen-begnadend.
Ihr Lichtes-Geister
Lasset vom Osten befeuern,
Was durch den Westen sich formet;
Dieses spricht:
In dem Christus wird Leben der Tod.
Das hören die Geister in Ost, West, Nord, Süd:
Menschen mögen es hören.

Menschenseele!
Du lebest im ruhenden Haupte,
Das dir aus Ewigkeitsgründen
Die Weltengedanken erschliesset:
Übe *Geist-Erschauen*
In Gedanken-Ruhe,
Wo die ew'gen Götterziele
Welten-Wesens-Licht
Dem eignen Ich
Zu freiem Wollen
Schenken;
Und du wirst wahrhaft *denken*
In Menschen-Geistes-Gründen.

Denn es walten des Geistes Weltgedanken
Im Weltenwesen Licht-erflehend.
Ihr Seelen-Geister
Lasset aus den Tiefen erbitten,
Was in den Höhen erhöret wird;
Dieses spricht:
In des Geistes Weltgedanken erwachet die Seele.
Das hören die Geister in Ost, West, Nord, Süd:
Menschen mögen es hören.

In der Zeiten Wende
Trat das Welten-Geistes-Licht
In den irdischen Wesensstrom;
Nacht-Dunkel
Hatte ausgewaltet;
Taghelles Licht
Erstrahlte in Menschenseelen;
Licht,
Das erwärmet
Die armen Hirtenherzen;
Licht,
Das erleuchtet
Die weisen Königshäupter.

Göttliches Licht,
Christus-Sonne,
Erwärme
Unsere Herzen;
Erleuchte
Unsere Häupter;

Dass gut werde,
Was wir
Aus Herzen gründen,
Was wir
Aus Häuptern
Zielvoll führen,
Wollen.

Further Reading

F. W. Zeylmans van Emmichoven, *The Foundation Stone* (Temple Lodge Publishing 2002)

Rudolf Grosse, *The Christmas Foundation, Beginning of a New Cosmic Age* (Steiner Book Centre 1984)

Rudolf Steiner, *The Christmas Conference for the Foundation of the General Anthroposophical Society 1923/1924* (Anthroposophic Press/Rudolf Steiner Press 1990). This volume contains facsimiles of Rudolf Steiner's notations on the blackboard.

Sergei O. Prokofieff, *Rudolf Steiner and the Founding of the New Mysteries* (Temple Lodge Publishing 1994).

May Human Beings Hear It, The Mystery of the Christmas Conference (Temple Lodge Publishing 2004)

About the Author

RUDOLF STEINER (1861–1925) called his spiritual philosophy 'anthroposophy', meaning 'wisdom of the human being'. As a highly developed seer, he based his work on direct knowledge and perception of spiritual dimensions. He initiated a modern and universal 'science of spirit', accessible to anyone willing to exercise clear and unprejudiced thinking.

From his spiritual investigations Steiner provided suggestions for the renewal of many activities, including education (both general and special), agriculture, medicine, economics, architecture, science, philosophy, religion and the arts. Today there are thousands of schools, clinics, farms and other organizations involved in practical work based on his principles. His many published works feature his research into the spiritual nature of the human being, the evolution of the world and humanity, and methods of personal development. Steiner wrote some 30 books and delivered over 6,000 lectures across Europe. In 1924 he founded the General Anthroposophical Society, which today has branches throughout the world.